1975

CONNOISSEUR'S LIBRARY

Glass
Geoffrey Wills

ORBIS PUBLISHING · LONDON

Contents

Designed and produced by Harriet Bridgeman Limited

© Istituto Geografico de Agostini, Novara 1973
Revised English Edition © Orbis Publishing Limited, London 1975
Printed in Italy by IGDA, Officine Grafiche, Novara
ISBN 0 85613 193 8

The origins of glass

Glass is a substance with innumerable uses as well as some qualities that are unique. It is brittle and hard, can be either transparent or opaque, and it is nowadays such a familiar material that very few people trouble to think what it is or why and how it was made. Undoubtedly glass came into being because of mankind's desire to imitate Nature, in this instance the colourless stone named rock-crystal, which is a pure form of the mineral silica.

As with many other everyday things, the origins of glass go back so far in history that they are now forgotten, and all that remains is legend. Two thousand years ago the Roman historian Pliny wrote down what he knew of the matter, and he was no doubt recording what had been repeated for countless centuries. Pliny's story was that some mariners or traders voyaging in the Mediterranean had the misfortune to be shipwrecked at the mouth of a river in Syria. They managed to scramble ashore and one of the first things they did was to light a fire with which to prepare a meal, but they could find no stones suitable for raising the cooking-pot above the flames.

It must be presumed they brought both the pot and its contents from the wreck, which, by coincidence, held a cargo of natron, a type of soda. Some lumps of the material were rescued and made an excellent trivet, the meal was cooked and eaten and then it was noticed that where the fire had blazed was a shiny deposit. This was crude glass, formed by the action of heat fusing the sand of the shore with the soda.

Basically, that is what occurs when glass is made now, although from time to time modifications have been introduced. Silica, in the form of sand or suitable stone, is fused with an alkali: the latter can be either soda or potash.

It is generally agreed that glass-making began in one of the countries of the eastern Mediterranean. Although the earliest surviving examples have been discovered in Egypt, it is thought that the art reached there from Asia Minor and that Egyptian craftsmen learned by imitation. It was a course of events that was repeated by one nation after another all over the world.

Whereas glass was at first used to counterfeit rock-crystal, the Egyptians had a particular liking for turquoise

and this was the stone they copied. Many examples of their ancient glass, some of them four thousand years old, are coloured turquoise-blue, while others are yellow or dark blue. They were limited by their knowledge and skill, and the articles they made were of small size. In most instances a string-like thread of hot glass was wound round a core of sand and clay. After the piece had cooled, it was carefully re-heated to fuse the 'strands' together and the core was chipped out. The process is a simple one, and specimens survive that still retain inside them traces of the core.

The first big advance in glass-making came about sometime in the first century AD, when an anonymous genius took an iron tube, dipped one end into a pot of molten glass and blew down it from the other. With the glass bubble that was made the art of glass-blowing had been discovered.

From that date onwards there was no lack of large and small bottles, vases and other hollow vessels, many of them made in Syria, Egypt or Rome, which were sent to all parts of the Roman Empire. In some countries there were local glass-houses, but in others, including England, almost all wants were imported. The glass-makers of Italy and Alexandria were highly competent: it has been said with truth that little or nothing made in modern times would have proved beyond the resources of the Mediterranean craftsmen of some two thousand years ago.

The Middle Ages

The fall of the Empire was followed by several centuries of stagnation during which the majority of the inhabitants of Europe were so busy fighting one another that they had little time to spare for peaceful arts.

The little glass-making that took place during this period was on a small scale, conducted by groups of men working near forests. From them they obtained the essential fuel for heating the components, as well as the alkali: potash from the ashes of burnt bracken. The impurity of the materials was matched by rough-and-ready workmanship; surviving specimens are not only scarce but more historically interesting than they are artistic. Small-sized drinking-vessels and bottles of German origin were decorated with applied blobs of glass, known as 'prunts', which were made to resemble flat raspberries or to form

BOWL FORMS

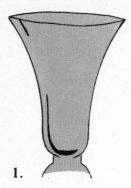

1.

2.

3.

4.

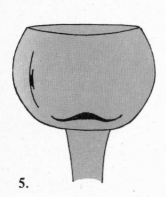

5.

6.

7.

8.

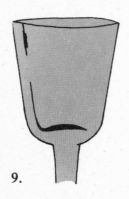

9.

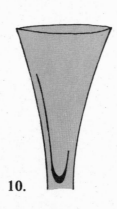

10.

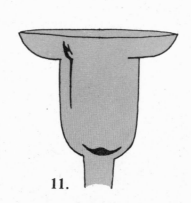

11.

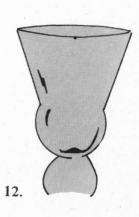

12.

1. Bell
2. Waisted
3. Bucket
4. Conical

5. Cup
6. Ogee
7. Hexagonal
8. Ovoid

9. Round Funnel
10. Trumpet
11. Saucer Topped
12. Thistle

sharp points. When these points were curled over they resembled animals' trunks, and they acquired the name of *Rüsselbecher*: literally, 'elephants' trunk beakers'. The German variety of the green-and-brown-tinted ware is known as *Waldglas* (forest-glass) and the French as *verre de fougère* (bracken-glass).

In contrast, the making of glass continued on a sophisticated level in the East, in the countries of the Moslem Empire of which Egypt was a part. Excavations carried out in modern times have uncovered evidence of the types of decoration current at different periods. Vases, bottles and bowls were shaped while still molten by means of pincers; ornament was applied by trailing strands of contrastingly-coloured glass over the surface of an article and cutting was practised. This last technique had for long been used for semi-precious stones and was employed on glass by the Romans and Egyptians.

Alexandrian craftsmen were especially adept at the work, the tradition no doubt having been passed on to them. Compared with the perfection of the first-century Portland Vase, made of two layers of glass of which the upper one was cut through to form the pattern, the later work is crude. This famous vase, now in the British Museum, London, is probably the best-known example of Roman glass and has probably never been excelled as a *tour de force*.

Cutting was performed by means of wheels of sandstone, or some other abrasive stone, fed with a constant flow of water and turned by a treadle. Other wheels were of metal fed with sand and water, and for polishing they were made of tin or wood. The work relied principally on the eye of the craftsman, and a mistake usually meant a ruined article; once a cut had been made it could seldom be removed or altered satisfactorily.

Most typical of Islamic, or Moslem, glass is the use of colour, either for the body of the article or for its ornamentation. In the latter case, enamels composed of coloured glasses with a comparatively low melting-point were painted on clear or tinted pieces and fixed permanently in the heat of a kiln. Much of the work reached a very high standard; among surviving specimens are a number of shaped lamps made to hang in mosques in commemoration of dead notables. Usually they bear lines from the Koran as well as a dedicatory inscription written in beautifully drawn letters, and it is possible to date them fairly closely. The best were executed in the thirteenth and fourteenth centuries and, while two examples are recorded with the signature of their painter, the others are unsigned. Because they were hung high up and normally well out of reach, their preservation was ensured and most of the lamps remained where they had been first placed until well into the nineteenth century.

Glass in the Venetian Republic

In time, however, the western world began to recover from its apathy and the Venetian Republic took control of the Mediterranean and much of the trade dependent on sea-borne traffic. The prosperity of Venice attracted

Above: Bottle in the shape of a fish, Egyptian, from El-Amarna. Late eighteenth dynasty (1580–1350 BC). Opaque core-formed glass, fish fully fashioned in the round with hollow body. Below: Amphoriskos, Greek. Second century BC. Core-formed glass with a translucent blue body and opaque-white trailing. (British Museum, London)

craftsmen from farther east, and among them were Syrian glass-makers. They established themselves first in the city, but, after some disastrous fires caused by their furnaces, they were banished to the comparative safety of the nearby island of Murano.

There, the immigrants taught their skills to local men, and together they evolved the wares that duly earned an international reputation for Venetian glass. Not only did they devise fresh shapes and colours, which were really variations on those known earlier and then forgotten, but they were able to improve on the quality of the material. Also, they achieved the distinction of producing a glass that was considerably clearer and less tinted than could be made elsewhere.

For their silica the Venetians relied upon supplies of white pebbles from the beds of the rivers Po and Ticino, in Italy, and these they combined with soda-bearing ash from sea-plants. The impurities that had for so long marred the clarity of the finished product were neutralized by the addition of small quantities of manganese oxide, and this resulted in what was then accepted as a close approximation to the coveted rock-crystal.

The Muranese makers formed themselves into guilds according to the types of goods in which they specialized, and the workers were strictly controlled. Above all, they were absolutely forbidden to seek employment outside the country, and there were threats of dire punishment for any who transgressed.

Despite the restrictions imposed on them, there was a steady trickle of men who ventured across the Republic's borders seeking their fortunes by assisting the establishment of glass-houses farther afield. They settled in Antwerp, Liège, Amsterdam and Middelburg and Maastricht in The Netherlands; others went to England, France, Spain and Portugal. Wares made in these places all owed their inspiration, if not to the actual hands of Venetian-born immigrant craftsmen, then certainly to imported wares. These were copied closely so that at this distance of time it is often difficult to distinguish between specimens made in Murano and those from elsewhere.

An exception is German glass for which potash, obtained from wood-ash, was employed. The ample forests found in many parts of Germany and in the neighbouring country of Bohemia supplied both the fuel and the alkali for the glass. The craft was often allied with the skill of the natives as lapidaries and carvers: a skill that showed itself in the fashioning of wood, stone, ivory and other substances. Sometimes the glass was painted in bright enamels, the technique probably originating in Bavaria and becoming established in other areas. A speciality was the making of large drinking-glasses painted with elaborate coats of arms, many of which bear seventeenth-century dates. While some examples are neatly executed, the majority are attractive only for their colourful appearance and the surprising fact that they have survived the passage of time undamaged.

Cutting and colouring

Caspar Lehmann, who lived between 1570 and 1622, was responsible for reviving the art of glass-cutting and bringing it back to the state at which the Romans had left it. He was the first in a long line of such craftsmen. In order to give more scope to their skill, experiments were made to devize a glass of greater clarity than was normal, with thicker walls that could withstand deep cutting.

Most of the seventeenth- and eighteenth-century German glass that has been preserved was made for ceremonial purposes. As in silver, tall cups and covers were especially popular, the glass ones being modelled on metal prototypes with cutting and engraving taking the place of embossing and other forms of decoration.

One group of Bohemian cutters became extremely skilled at producing double-walled glasses known as *Zwischengoldgläser*: literally, 'gold-between glasses'. A special glass with an outward-sloping bowl, either a beaker or a goblet, was decorated on the outside with black outlines filled with gold and silver leaf; this was covered with a close-fitting outer glass and a disc put in the base. The whole was cemented together so as to make it waterproof and protect the ornamentation. So cleverly was this done that the joins in the glasses are almost invisible and the method of decorating proves a puzzle to the innocent.

Towards the end of the seventeenth century attempts were made to improve the colours of glass then available. A chemist named Johann Kunckel, of Potsdam, was successful in producing a deep ruby colour which has been described as resembling 'red currant or red ink'. It is not to be confused with the nineteenth-century ruby-coloured glass that came from Bohemia and Stourbridge.

Experiments in England

In England, the origins of glass-making in modern times may be said to date from the early thirteenth century when, in the year 1226, a man named Laurence established a furnace near Chiddingfold, on the borders of Surrey and Sussex. It was a well-timbered area so that, with the addition of suitable sand, the necessary raw materials were readily available. Laurence had crossed the Channel from France and he was the first of many of his compatriots to do the same. They supplied principally window-glass, plain and coloured, as well as simple vessels, their output being comparable to the *verre de fougère* of their native land and the *Waldglas* of Germany.

Attempts at making more attractive wares did not take place until 1549, when Edward VI permitted eight Venetians to come from Antwerp and set up a glasshouse in London. They failed at their task and within a few years seven had returned whence they came, the eighth going to Liège. Fifteen years later there was a further essay, when Cornelius de Lannoy came to teach his art 'as practised in the Netherlands', but even after three years he failed and it would seem he was simply an impostor.

Jean Carré, who had arranged the visit of the first group of Venetians, then tried again. In 1570 he brought over more men, setting them to work in premises near the Tower of London. On this occasion Carré not only introduced more satisfactory craftsmen, but he was responsible for their adopting the style of furnace used in Murano and

The Portland Vase, Roman. Late first century BC, or first century AD. Mould-blown cameo-cut glass. (British Museum, London)

6

7

Mosque lamp, Syrian. AD 1330–45. Enamelled and gilded glass. (British Museum, London)

hitherto unknown in England, as well as the type of alkali favoured there, known as 'barilla'. It came from the coastal regions of Spain and was derived from the plant named 'glasswort'. The dried and fruited bushes were set alight, 'and when the flame comes to the berries they melt and come into an azure liquor'. After an interval the juice congealed into a blue-coloured stone, 'which is so hard that it is scarcely malleable', but, more to the point, it contained soda that was ideal for glass-making.

Jacopo Verzelini and a royal patent

Carré died in 1572 and his place as manager of the concern was taken over by one of the Venetians, Jacopo Verzelini. To him are attributed on strong grounds a small number of surviving drinking-glasses. However, soon after he had taken charge Verzelini suffered a setback: in September 1575 the glass-house in Crutched Friars, near the Tower, caught fire and only the bare walls remained. Undaunted, he recommenced operations in Broad Street, also in the City and no great distance from the scene of the recent disaster.

At the same time he applied to Queen Elizabeth I for a patent 'for the makinge of drinkinge glasses such as be accustomably made in the towne of Murano'. This he was granted for a period of twenty-one years provided he

taught English workers the art, and in return all imports were prohibited: a ban which was probably not applied with any seriousness.

The glasses now attributed to Jacopo Verzelini's glass-house are nine in number and are mostly in museums in London, Paris and the United States. All are goblets, with bowls of various shapes, and eight of them are distinctively decorated with designs engraved (or scratched) by means of a diamond-point. The ninth has ornament of a comparable style but in gold. Some are initialled, others bear names in full, all are dated between 1577 and 1590 and two show the motto of the Pewterers' Company of London: 'In God is all my Trust'.

This last feature has led to a proposal that the engraving was executed by a Frenchman, Antony de Lisle, or de Lysle, who was a pewter-engraver known to have been living in London at the relevant time. The actual goblets differ little, if at all, from those being made on the Continent at that date but, with craftsmen coming and going and interchanging ideas, this is not unexpected. It is improbable that proof will ever be forthcoming that the nine glasses are not of English make, so it is reasonable to suppose they were the work of Verzelini.

Following Verzelini's death in 1606, a number of other men successively held the glass-making monopoly, but very little of what they produced has been identified. Their activities are known from patents and other documents, and it is assumed that the vessels they made are indistinguishable from imported examples.

The earliest wine-bottles

The middle years of the seventeenth century saw the country in the turmoil of civil war, and the rule of Oliver Cromwell which followed its termination was not encouraging to industrial enterprize. Such glass as was then made was probably for general use, while anything more luxurious and decorative would have had to be brought from across the Channel. However, despite the political upheavals, this period witnessed the introduction of an object, now a commonplace but of which old specimens are of great interest to collectors: the wine-bottle.

Its introduction has been attributed to Sir Kenelm Digby, an author and diplomatist whose words and actions aroused much comment during his lifetime. Digby's claim to have been responsible for the wine-bottle was apparently not made by him, but by another, and then only in 1662, thirty years after the event was alleged to have occurred. Bottles of one kind and another had been known and used from the earliest times, though perhaps hitherto their use had been confined to medicinal and other purposes, for which they were normally of small size.

The glass used for the first wine-bottles was of the common green-coloured type made originally by the forest-workers. Being completely hand made, each bottle was individual in external appearance and it was not possible to make them of a standard capacity. Their use was at first confined to the few, many of whom had the bottles made with a mark of ownership on each one. This was achieved by simply putting a blob of molten glass on the partly finished bottle and impressing it with a circular brass seal.

The size of the seals is usually about one inch in diameter and they are engraved variously. Most of them bear the name of the owner, with or without that of his residence, and a date; others show a crest or coat of arms; some have initials alone with a date.

A further variety embodies devices and were sometimes made for owners of inns. A surviving specimen shows the figure of a mermaid with the words 'ANTHONY HALL IN OXFORD' and the date of 1685; this has been traced to the Mermaid Inn in that city, where it was owned by successive members of the Hall family between about 1660 and 1690. They and other publicans doubtless supplied wines in their bottles to the colleges of the University, but in time the custom changed and many of the colleges had their own bottles made.

Because a proportion of them bear dates, it has been possible to trace changes in their shape over the years. At first, in about 1650, each was given a tall neck rising from a globular body with just below the rim a raised ring of glass: the string-rim used to retain the string holding in place the cover of paper or parchment. In due course corks were employed and the string-rim was raised level with the rim to give strength in a vulnerable area.

By about 1690 the shape had altered to a short neck above a squat body, which gives a pleasing appearance although it is not easy to grip or to pour from. From about 1715 the body became cylindrical and, within the ensuing thirty to forty years, the shape of the modern bottle evolved. A simple hinged mould came into use early in the nineteenth century, and thenceforward it was possible to produce any number of bottles which were standardized in

Left: Wineglass by Jacopo Verzelini (1522–1606). Dated 1581. Diamond-engraved glass. (Victoria and Albert Museum, London) Right: Bowl with the seal of George Ravenscroft (1618–81). c.1680. (Private Collection)

in the shape as well as in the capacity of the bottle.

The modern shape of bottle came into being because the eighteenth-century Englishman found port wine agreeable to his taste and to his pocket for, from 1703, it was dutiable at a much lower rate than French wines. Port was found to mature when it was carefully kept, and the bottles containing it not only took up less space when stacked on their sides but the corks remained airtight when moist from contact with the contents.

The earliest surviving dated bottle is one of 1657, found in Northampton and now in Northampton Central Museum and Art Gallery, while a seal alone of 1652 is in the London Museum. Bottles of these dates, and also later ones, feature a pronounced 'kick up' beneath the base: a depression formed deliberately during the making. One part of the process involved holding the semi-finished article by means of an iron rod (pontil), which was stuck to the base with a small lump of molten glass. When the pontil was removed it left a jagged scar, the pontil-mark, and this was pushed inwards clear of the base so that the bottle stood steadily and did not make scratches.

A large proportion of seventeenth- and eighteenth-century bottles were made at Bristol, which was also a convenient port for exportation. Many were sent to America, where excavations at Colonial Williamsburg, Virginia, and elsewhere, have revealed thousands of

9

fragments of smashed bottles, some complete examples and many seals. In some instances they have been traced by names or initials on them to their original settler-owners.

Ravenscroft and 'flint glass'

With the restoration of the monarchy and the accession to the throne of Charles II a noticeable change in thought took place. His coronation coincided with an upsurge throughout Europe of interest in scientific phenomena. In England, among many other things, attention turned to improving the quality of glass. This came about not only from a desire to make a better product, but to save expenditure abroad by producing an acceptable substitute for the goods of which the Venetians had a virtual monopoly.

As a first step towards achieving this end, the Glass Sellers' Company, which had obtained its Charter in 1664, engaged the services of George Ravenscroft. Already operating a glass-house in London, he petitioned in 1673 for a patent for 'a particular sort of Christalline Glass resembling Rock Crystal not formerly used or exercised in

Sir Thomas Saunders Sebright, Bt., Sir John Bland, Bt. and two other gentlemen smoking and drinking in a painting by B. Ferrers. 1720. (Christie Manson and Woods, London)

this our Kingdome'. Members of the Company were shown samples of the material and decided to establish Ravenscroft at Henley-on-Thames. There, far from prying eyes, he could conduct his experiments without hindrance.

Ravenscroft tried using English flints in place of the Italian pebbles, powdering the flints by heating and then grinding them, and instead of barilla he used potash. To aid the fusion of the mixture he added some lead oxide (probably red lead), and in due course the flints were supplanted by sand. The term 'flint glass' became current and, despite the fact that it was only briefly applicable, it has remained in use to the present day.

The first glass produced by Ravenscroft had a tendency to crizzling: to develop a network of very fine internal cracks resembling a spider's web and producing a semi-opacity. In extreme cases, a vessel would become moist on the surface and 'weep', until it finally decomposed altogether and crumbled. By June 1676 the Company, which was responsible for the maker's entire output, announced that the trouble had been rectified. In order that buyers could identify the now-perfected glass, Ravenscroft was permitted to place his personal mark on each specimen. He did this by applying a small blob of glass, about one quarter of an inch in diameter, and impressing it in the manner of sealing a letter with a tiny raven's head in relief. It was a miniature version of the seals placed on wine-bottles, although on the latter the seal was that of the owner and not the maker.

About a score of these marked articles have been recorded, their number including bowls, drinking-glasses and ewers. Some of them show traces of crizzling that has developed during the past three centuries; all are made of Ravenscroft's lead glass. The material is quite different from the old soda or potash, lead-free, glass, for it is not only heavier in the hand, but is much more brilliant. In appearance it has been aptly described as having 'a light-dispersing character that gave it a remarkable interior fire, especially in thick-walled vessels'.

Predictably, Ravenscroft's pieces were made in imitation of those imported from Venice which had hitherto monopolized the market and were familiar as well as fashionable. The majority of the lead-glass articles of that time are thin walled, yet even so they are often superior in appearance to their rivals and quite obviously made of a material with different characteristics. Soon, with a general adoption in England of the new glass, it began to dictate the styles in which it was shown at its most effective.

The Venetian glass mixture (or 'metal') was of a thin consistency when molten, tending to cool quickly, and it was blown into very fragile forms with the thinnest possible walls. The English metal was less fluid and cooled at a slower rate. It resisted efforts to blow it thinly; a fact that ensured the revelation of its full beauty. This was exploited by successive generations of glass-makers from the late seventeeth century onwards, giving their wares a fame that reached far beyond the shores of the British Isles.

Eighteenth-century drinking-glasses

The great majority of surviving eighteenth-century English glass takes the form of drinking-vessels; above all, wine-glasses. Their patterns over the years echo the changes in style that took place in silver, furniture and other domestic wares, and at the same time they are evidence of the increasing luxury of daily life as the century progressed.

At first in Queen Anne's reign, glasses tended to be tall and heavily made, with no sparing of the material. Bowls were of several forms, and stems likewise varied in design. They were built up by craftsmen combining differently shaped sections, some of which were contrived to enclose an air-bubble, and their finished effect depended solely on the maker's skill and judgment. Thus, each one differed from another and, even when two or more of apparently matching pattern are compared, it will be found that there are variations in the individual specimens.

Up to about 1745 it was usual to provide a glass with what is named a 'folded foot', a double thickness round the edge where the rim was turned under during manufacture. It protected a vulnerable area from chipping and

Glass-makers at work, printed in London. 1747. (Mansell Collection, London)

must have saved innumerable specimens from such damage. The centre of the foot was invariably domed for the same reasons that a bottle was given its kick-up, so as to have the pontil-mark where it would neither cause scratches nor make the article unsteady. When, towards the end of the eighteenth century, it became the practice to grind flat the pontil-mark, there was no longer any necessity to dome the foot and it became flat.

The early, simple air-bubble in the stem was often elongated to became tear shaped, and a development of this led to a group of the bubbles being formed into what is termed an 'air twist'. The glass rod enclosing the bubbles was cleverly manipulated so that each globule of air became a silvery-looking strand and these were twisted into spirals. The popularity of air-twist stems dated from the mid-eighteenth century and was followed by the practice of enclosing in the clear stem opaque-white or coloured glass rods, which were treated in a manner similar to the bubbles. In both instances a great variety of patterns was attainable, and modern collectors compete for the rarer

11

English wine-bottles with owners' seals. Eighteenth century. (Christie, Manson and Woods, London)

types as well as for the comparatively commonplace ones. Of the colours employed, yellow is the scarcest, but green and purple are almost equally seldom found.

It has been argued that the tax on glass first imposed in 1745 had an effect on production as well as on design. Levied on the weight of materials used, it led to the manufacture of vessels with thinner walls than formerly, to the sacrifice of the very practical folded foot, and possibly it also stimulated the employment of ornament as compensation for the lack of metal. Although previously they had been far from unknown, various types of decorated glassware became more common from that time onwards.

Cutting, which perhaps became fashionable with the arrival in London in 1714 of the first of the Hanoverian kings, George I, was foreshadowed a few years earlier. A newspaper of 1709 printed a notice stating that:

'There is lately brought over a great parcel of very fine German Cut and Carved Glasses. viz. Jellies, Wine and Water Tumblers, Beer and Wine Glasses with Covers, and divers other sorts. The like hath not been exposed to public sale before.'

The term 'cutting' is applied to faceting and slicing, whereas more delicate patterns and inscriptions, although executed in a similar manner, are referred to as engraving. In the mid-century the latter was effectively employed for ornamenting wineglasses and decanters produced for

adherents to the cause of the Jacobites. Such articles have been sought by many collectors during the past few decades and still excite interest and keen competition when they become available.

The Jacobites held that the true heir to the throne of England was the son of the exiled Catholic king, James II: this son was James Francis Edward Stuart, known as 'The Old Pretender'. When his father died in France in 1701 Louis XIV declared the boy, then aged thirteen, James III of England and James VIII of Scotland. An unsuccessful attempt to start a revolt in Scotland was foiled by the English fleet and bad weather, and then the Pretender established his Court at Scone, Perthshire, where he stayed for under a year before fleeing back to France. Later he went to Rome, married and duly had a son, Charles Edward Stuart, 'The Young Pretender'. The latter also made a landing in Scotland, whence he marched with a small army into England, but he was driven back and decisively beaten at the Battle of Culloden in April 1746. Despite their conspicuous lack of success, the number of surviving eighteenth-century Jacobite glasses suggests that both Pretenders had no lack of sympathizers.

As the Pretenders' cause was a treasonable one, decorative allusion to it on the glasses was often disguised and the deciphering of symbols, and suspected symbols, has involved considerable argument. The most frequently employed was a rose branch with a flower and one or more buds, which has been said to represent the English Crown – the flower – with the two Pretenders as buds. Alternative emblems, used singly or in conjunction with others, included a thistle, a star, a bird and a bee. A number of cryptic inscriptions also appear, some in English, but mostly they are in Latin. In the last category are: *Fiat* (May it happen: *i.e.* the hoped-for ascent to the throne of England); *Redi* (Return) and *Revirescit* (He grows strong again: *i.e.* the House of Stuart).

Proclaiming their message more openly, some glasses bear portraits of the Young Pretender, while others are finely diamond-engraved with all or some of the verses of the Jacobite anthem, the concluding lines of which refer to bringing home 'the King who hath best right to reign, It is the only thing can save the nation'. Because the inscription invariably ends with the word 'Amen', the glasses, of which under twenty genuine ones are known to exist, are known as 'Amen Glasses'. It should be noted that forgeries of these, and of other glasses with Jacobite decoration, have been made and could prove deceptive.

Engraved glasses were made also for the rival Williamites, who commemorated the success of the Protestant William III at the Battle of the Boyne in 1690. The King is shown, usually on horseback, and the accompanying inscriptions are in English. Although examples sometimes bear the date of the Battle, this does not refer to the year in which they were made, which was usually about half a century or more later. The Williamite movement was (and still is) strong in parts of Ireland and it is possible that the engraving was executed in Dublin, where a glass-house advertized in 1752 that it could supply such work 'of any kind or pattern ... toasts or any flourish whatsoever'.

The use of engraving was by no means confined to political and religious sentiment: it was used sometimes to inscribe a name and date, a miniature landscape or whatever would please the buyer. Alternatively, decoration was carried out in coloured or white enamels, or in gold, the latter seldom surviving the passage of time without blemish owing to its delicate nature. The finest of the enamelling was done by members of the Beilby family, of Newcastle upon Tyne, who were active there from about 1760 to 1778. William and Mary Beilby, brother and sister, worked sometimes together and sometimes individually, but only rarely did they sign their productions. They used wineglasses, decanters and bowls made at a local manufactory, whose wares were distinguished by their clarity and shapes.

Newcastle glass enjoyed a reputation outside England and was exported to the Netherlands as well as elsewhere in Europe. A number of Dutch decorators employed it, for their work, which they performed by means of a splinter of diamond held in a rod. The rod was tapped with a light hammer and the resulting pattern of tiny dots and dashes was a 'stipple engraving' of great refinement.

Glass was made and also exported at another port, Bristol. Although all kinds were manufactured, including bottles, the city is especially remembered for a blue-coloured glass. 'Bristol Blue' is stated to be of a distinctive colour and is often described as if it was made exclusively in that place; neither statement is true. A few examples bear the mark in gilt 'I Jacobs, Bristol' and were the work of Isaac Jacobs, of The Non-Such Flint Glass Manufactory, which he established in 1805, but the origin of unmarked pieces can only be assumed.

Bristol was at one time considered to have been the source of an opaque-white glass resembling porcelain which is now attributed to one or more places in south Staffordshire. Pieces were decorated in colours or gold with subjects similar to those found on chinaware of the time. James Giles, who had premises in Berwick Street, London, and elsewhere, has for long been known as a buyer and decorator of various makes of eighteenth-century porcelain and has recently been discovered to have painted glass as well.

Cut, as distinct from engraved, ornament became increasingly popular after the middle years of the century. A knowledge of what was available for purchase is to be gained from an advertisement in a newspaper of 1752, in which a London dealer announced that he stocked:

'Flint Glasses, brilliant Lustres [chandeliers], Branches [candelabra], Candlesticks, Dishes, Plates, Bowls, Basons, Cups and Covers, Saucers, Saltcellars, cut Bottles, Decanters, Rummers, cut and flowered, Desart Glasses of all sorts; Scollop'd or engraved Salvers . . . Cruets and Castors; curious Lamps; Wash-hand Glasses [finger-bowls], most curiously engraved new-fashion'd or scollop'd; and finest polish'd Mugs, and Pitchers, Turkish-fashion Diamond-cut and Brilliant polish'd.'

Glass-making in Ireland

In the 1750s wineglasses were given facet-cut stems, similar ornament sometimes being applied to the upper surface and rim of the foot. From about the same time simple faceting on other articles began to develop slowly into elaborate cross-cutting, reaching a peak of complexity in the 1820s. Such work required vessels with extra thick walls so that the cuts could be made deep, but as the years passed the glass tax was increased and in 1781 makers found a way of circumventing it. This was done by producing their wares in Ireland, where they would be free of any tax and could be exported to England in addition to being sent farther afield. A number of glass-houses were started in Waterford and other towns, staffed in the main by English craftsmen and producing goods largely indistinguishable from those they had made in their native land.

Much has been written about the characteristics of old Irish-made glass, supposedly recognizable by its grey-blue tint and its clear ringing tone when smartly rapped. These theories, and others, cannot be substantiated, however, and the only pieces of which the origin can be proved beyond any dispute are decanters, finger-bowls and jugs with the names of their makers in raised letters beneath their bases. This was done at Waterford, Cork and a few other places.

Usually attributed to Waterford are large-sized oval, round or canoe-shaped bowls for fruit or salad. They are raised on pedestals with moulded feet; some examples have the bowl rim curled under and are known as 'turnover bowls'. All the bowls are remarkable for the weight of glass, as well as for the precision and variety of their cut decoration.

A further effort to produce cheap glassware by saving the duty payable was resorted to at a manufactory set up at Nailsea, near Bristol. Articles were made from bottle-glass, which was taxed at a lower rate than other kinds, and a simple decoration was applied in the form of spattered blobs of opaque white. Makers in other areas made similar wares, but it is seldom possible to state where they came from. As well as pieces in green-tinted glass, others in clear metal with coloured stripes and splashes were made at Nailsea. They include such things as rolling-pins, witch-balls, hand-bells and walking-sticks. Similar pieces and others of greater elaboration, such as fully rigged sailing-ships, are sometimes referred to as 'friggers': the glass-maker's term for pieces made in his spare time.

Hyalith, Lithyalin and Millefiori

The early decades of the nineteenth century saw further glass-making innovations from Central Europe, where a number of new types of glass and styles of ornamentation were devized. The earlier *Zwischengoldglas* technique was revived and adapted by J. J. Mildner who, with infinite care, inset shaped and decorated glass plaques into the walls of vessels. He had his workshop at Gutenbrunn, in Lower Austria, and some of his surviving work bears the name of the town as well as his signature and a date. In exceptional instances Mildner enclosed between layers of glass a miniature painted on vellum, while an unknown crafts-man similarly arranged tiny scenes composed of glass, straw, coloured paper and other materials.

Coloured glasses of various kinds were produced in Bohemia. Josef Reider complimented his wife Anna by naming his green and yellow metals after her; respectively, *Annagrün* and *Annagelb*. Another maker, Count von Boquoy, evolved a stone-like material in a reddish colour and black which was named *'Hyalith'*. A rival to it was *Lithyalin*, from a factory at Blottendorf and, like the other introductions, this one enjoyed the flattery of imitation by numerous rivals.

Colouring was also obtained by giving clear glass one or more outer coatings of coloured metal or by applying a chemical stain to the surface. In both instances the outside could be cut through in a pattern, or to form 'windows' which could be painted, gilded or left clear. A ruby-stained ground was especially popular in the 1850s and later, and it is now often difficult to decide whether examples originated in Bohemia or in England at about the same date.

The technique of combining threads of white and colour with clear glass had been used in Roman times. It was revived in Murano and again practised in France in the nineteenth century, in the latter instance its most success-ful exploitation being the making of ornamental paper-weights. These clear glass domes enclosing coloured patterns were made at three manufactories: Baccarat, St. Louis and Clichy, and it is usually possible to distinguish the products of each. In some specimens one of the coloured ornaments, called 'canes', is composed of the initial letter or letters of the factory: 'B 1848' stands for Baccarat 1848, S.L. for St. Louis, while a Clichy origin is recognized by a rose in full bloom. Door-handles, bell-pulls and other objects were made in the same style, but the paperweights were, and remain, the most coveted of all.

The Baccarat and other French factories copied the English style of cutting, but also specialized in making a pastel-shade, semi-transparent glass known by the name of 'Opaline'. This was produced in many tints and was often mounted attractively in gilt bronze. Copies, which were rarely up to the standard of quality of the original, were made not only in Bohemia but in England.

In that country, the Worcestershire town of Stourbridge had gradually become the centre of the glass trade and, following the removal of the glass duty in 1845, it was able to compete on better terms with foreign makers. Not only was this done by copying or attempting to improve upon imported wares, but fiscal freedom allowed the introduc-tion of new ideas. Many of these were the result of an increased awareness of good design among a section of the public. Their cudgels were taken up by John Ruskin and others and resulted in a movement towards simple patterns and conscientious workmanship and against elaborate, meaningless design and machine-made goods. Inevitably, the reaction was rather too severe to last and, by the end of the nineteenth century, design again took second place in favour of execution.

In this instance the work was principally performed by hand and took the form of a revival of the Roman skill at cameo work, familiarly typified by the Portland Vase. The Vase presented a challenge that modern workers were keen to accept, and in 1873 a Stourbridge man, John Northwood, set to work on a task that took him three years to complete. Northwood did other work of the same kind and before long was being imitated by other craftsmen. At the height of the demand for cameo work there were hundreds of carvers of varying proficiency busily engaged in satisfying an eager market.

At the same period there was a call for hand-manipulated pieces that owed nothing to the cutting-wheel or any other tool. Japanese influence can often be detected in their shapes, and many of the vases and other items rely for much of their effect on the occurrence of bubbles and striations in the material.

The later years of the century saw the production of coloured and clear glass by mass-production methods. The process of press-moulding had been first devized in England, was developed and exploited in the United States and then returned whence it came. A regulated quantity of molten glass was placed in a shaped mould and a plunger lowered so that the glass was pressed into the mould. It was simple, quick and cheap; enormous quanti-ties could be turned out to suit the needs of the rapidly expanding population. The Newcastle area was the site of several factories making pressed glass and working twenty-four hours a day to meet the demand for their products.

Colonial American glass

Across the Atlantic Ocean there was little glass-making on any scale prior to the mid-eighteenth century. A factory in New Jersey conducted by Caspar Wistar and his son, Richard, between 1739 and 1780, made colour-striped and other wares in the Nailsea manner. Popularly attributed to Wistar workers in their spare time are blown articles decorated with coloured prunts and shaped, applied ornaments of 'lily-pad' form. Pieces in German style, roughly engraved as well as coloured, were made in Pennsylvania by Henry William Stiegel who, like Wistar, came to America from Germany, but again the output was

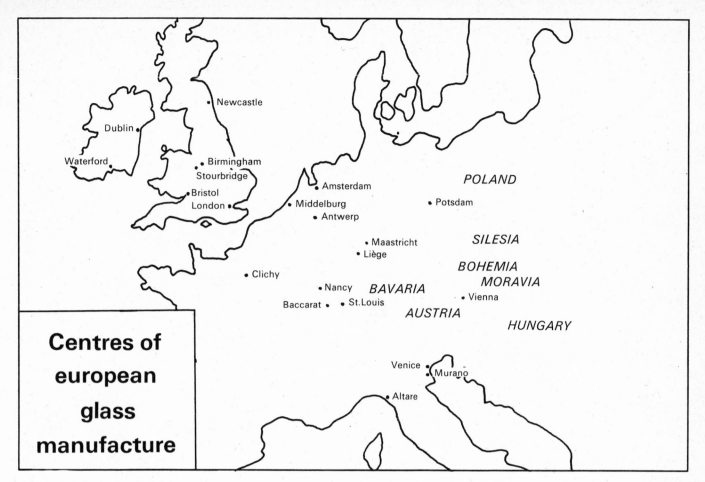

Centres of european glass manufacture

almost exclusively imitative of imported goods, and attributions are mostly no more than tentative. Other glass-houses have been recorded, in many cases started by men who had worked with Wistar or Stiegel, but few of them survived the turmoil of the War of Independence.

When once peace had been re-established, moves were afoot to start new industries that would once and for all free the country of imported wares. A new generation of glass-makers met the challenge, among their first successes being the introduction of press-moulding. While at first the process was employed to make cheap reproductions of Waterford-type cut glass, it later concentrated on what are called 'lacy' patterns, formed from bead-like raised dots.

A local speciality were hip-flasks, moulded with commemorative portraits and inscriptions, made at Zanesville, Ohio, and elsewhere. All the types of glass current in Europe were produced also in the States, not excepting patterned paperweights. Although attractive, they never managed to attain the perfection of the originals. Coloured glasses of various types, notably a yellow merging into pink known as 'Burmese', were developed and marketed in England and other countries.

Art Nouveau

A number of French manufacturers experimented with different methods of coating glass, which they then engraved and etched with acid. Prominent among them were Emile Gallé and the Daum brothers, all of whom came from the town of Nancy. They were notable for raising the status of the glass-maker to that of the painter, and their work, as well as that of others who attempted to rival them, was invariably signed. In many cases the signature almost becomes part of the decorative character of the piece.

Towards the close of the nineteenth century research was directed towards evolving types of glass with an iridescent surface, based in appearance on pieces that had been buried and then excavated. Austrian makers were prominent in such work, and the fashion quickly spread elsewhere. In New York, L. C. Tiffany, son of a well-known jeweller, established a highly successful glass manufactory on Long Island, where he produced a variety of fresh types of glass with which he achieved an international fame. His reading-lamps, particularly, whether in the form of wisteria or other shrubs, or patterned with large dragonflies, show a very early mastery of the problem of merging electric light agreeably into domestic surroundings. Tiffany's glass, with its arresting combinations of colours and its simple forms epitomizes the turn of the century, the Art Nouveau of the time and his own inventiveness. The ancient technique of working with glass paste, *pâte de verre*, was also revived at the end of the century and is associated with such names as Dammouse, Décorchement and Almeric Walter.

Then, as in the earliest times, glass-makers persisted in their search for new ideas, which were no sooner initiated than they were improved upon, imitated and cast aside in favour of something fresher. The same continues to occur today. The story of glass is still an exciting one of new techniques, improved materials and changing designs.

Glossary of terms

Air-twist stem. A type of stem used on English eighteenth-century drinking-glasses incorporating glass rods enclosing air-bubbles

Annealing. The process of strengthening flint glass by raising it to a high temperature and then allowing it to cool gradually

Baluster stem. A stem of short, pillar form, pure, inverted or knopped, used in English drinking-glasses of the late seventeenth and eighteenth centuries

Bristol Blue. A blue glass produced at several glass manufactories in the British Isles, but principally at Bristol

Cane. A rod of glass, sections of which are combined to form the patterns in *millefiori* glass

Crizzling. The clouding of glass by the formation of a network of cracks caused by a fault in the chemical make-up; Ravenscroft glass was particularly prone to crizzling

Façon de Venise. Glass vessels made throughout Europe in imitation of Venetian glass of the sixteenth and seventeenth centuries

Favrile. The trade name for art nouveau glass with an iridescent or lustred surface made by Tiffany

Finial. A decorative projection at the apex of a piece

Flint glass. A type of dense, heavy glass invented by George Ravenscroft; the flint was soon supplanted, but the term is retained to describe lead glass

Folded foot. A foot with a double thickness of glass at the edge where it is turned under in the course of manufacture; it serves to strengthen the glass at a vulnerable point

Forest glass. A clear green or brown glass made with potash derived from the ashes of burnt bracken; known as *Waldglas* in Germany and *verre de fougère* in France

Humpen. A cylindrical beaker of German or Bohemian origin

Hyalith. A black glass invented by Count von Buquoy in 1822 of which wares were made at the manufactory of Friedrich Egermann in Bohemia

Iridescence. A rainbow-like effect on the surface of ancient glass caused by weathering, achieved in the nineteenth century by artificial means

Kit Cat glass. A baluster-stem wineglass with a tall stem and outward curving bowl, so called because of its appearance in a painting by Kneller of members of the Kit Cat Club

Knop. A knob resembling a bud found particularly on stemmed drinking-glasses

Lithyalin. A marbled glass developed by Friedrich Egermann in Bohemia in the 1820s

Metal. Glass, the substance, in its unworked or worked state

Millefiori. A clear glass embedded with sections of coloured canes arranged in patterns, used particularly in France at Baccarat, Clichy and St. Louis in the manufacture of paperweights

Opaline glass. A translucent, opaque glass fashionable in France in the Empire period

Opaque-twist stem. An English drinking-glass stem containing spirals of opaque glass

Pontil. The metal rod to the end of which the glass article is attached during manufacture; when removed it often leaves a scar on the base of the vessel known as the 'pontil mark'

Prunt. A blob of glass applied as decoration

Zwischengoldglas. A glass, usually a tumbler, of double thickness with a layer of gold leaf sealed between the two

Bibliography

Barrington Haynes, E., *Glass Through the Ages*, Penguin Books, Harmondsworth 1959 (revised edition)

Davis, F., *The Country Life Book of Glass*, Country Life, London 1966

Harden, D. B., Painter, K. S., Pinder Wilson, R. H. and Tait, H., *Masterpieces of Glass*, Trustees of the British Museum, London 1968

Kämpfer, F. and Beyer, K. G., *Glass: A World History*, Studio Vista, London 1966

Middlemas, K., *Continental Coloured Glass*, Barrie and Jenkins, London 1971

Wills, G., *The Country Life Pocket Book of Glass*, Country Life, London 1966

Wilkinson, O. N., *Old Glass*, Benn, London 1968

Acknowledgements are due to the following for photographs used in this volume: Ashmolean Museum, Oxford: 25. André Berg: 101, 103. B.P.C. Publishing Ltd., London: 1, 5, 6, 10, 11, 12, 13, 14, 15, 16, 17, 18, 19, 20, 21, 22, 23, 24, 26, 27, 28, 29, 30, 31, 32, 33, 34, 35, 36, 37, 38, 39, 40, 41, 42, 44, 46, 47, 51, 52, 53, 54, 55, 56, 57, 58, 59, 60, 61, 62, 63, 64, 65, 67, 68, 69, 70, 74, 76, 83, 90, 91, 92, 93, 94, 95, 96, 97, 98, 99, 100, 106, 107, 108, 109, 110, 111, 112. British Museum, London: 7, 8, 43, 49, 50. Clevedon Court, Somerset: 87, 88, 89. Corning Museum of Glass, U.S.A.: 113, 114. Giraudon, Paris: 105. Kunstmuseum der Stadt, Dusseldorf: 4. Kunstindustrimuseet, Oslo: 85, 86. Patricia McCawley: 77, 78, 79, 80, 81, 82, 84. Novosti Press Agency, London: 66. Pilkington Glass Museum, St. Helens: 48. Sotheby & Co., London: 102, 104. Sotheby's Belgravia, London: 115, 116, 117, 118. Victoria & Albert Museum, London: 2, 3, 45, 71, 72, 73, 75. Line drawings: Lyle Publications, Worthing, Sussex.

1 *Manuscript miniature* showing glass-making, one of the twenty-eight illustrations to *The Travels of Sir John Mandeville*, Flemish or German. Fifteenth century (British Museum, London). The miniature illustrates the various stages in glass-making: at the top, digging for the raw materials; below, melting the frit (ground-up components), blowing and annealing, and removing the finished object from the furnace. The basic constituents of glass are silica – usually sand – and an alkali such as soda or potash.

2 *Green glass goblet*, Venice. *c.*1480 (Victoria and Albert Museum, London). Magnificent decoration resembling the glitter of precious stones was common on goblets made to commemorate a betrothal or marriage. This goblet has an enamelled portrait head and gilding on the foot.

3 *Beaker*, Venice. *c.*1490 (Victoria and Albert Museum, London). The enamelled decoration is of two mermen. Enamelling on glass was practised in Europe in the Middle Ages, to be revived in Venice in the mid-fifteenth century. At first it was executed on coloured glass (2), later on clear glass as here.

4

5

4 *Humpen* (a more or less cylindrical beaker) with enamelled decoration, Bohemian. 1594 (Kunstmuseum, Dusseldorf).

5 *Reichsadlerhumpen*, German. 1604 (Victoria and Albert Museum, London). A *Reichsadlerhumpen* is a beaker with the double-headed eagle and arms of the states of the Holy Roman Empire executed in enamelling.

6 *Enamelled Humpen*, Bohemian. 1680 (Museum of Arts and Crafts, Prague). This was presented to Caspar Steiner of Volpersdorf by Christian Preussler, one of a large and famous family of glass-makers in Zeilberg. The decoration of the *Humpen* depicts their glassworks at Zeilberg.

7 *Footed beaker*, decorated by Johann Schaper, Nuremberg. *c.*1660–70 (British Museum, London). The decorative technique employed here is known as *Schwarzlot* and consists of black enamelling with highlights of gold and sometimes red. The portrait is of John George II, Elector of Saxony.

8 *Stangenglas* (tall glass), Southern Netherlands or Rhineland. Late sixteenth or early seventeenth century (British Museum, London). This is a late example of *Waldglas*, or forest glass, with raspberry prunts. The forests of northern Europe supplied the fuel for glass-making and alkali was obtained from burnt bracken.

9 *Covered goblet*, Nuremberg. Late seventeenth century (British Museum, London). The goblet, of combined clear and coloured glass, is surmounted by a knop with a strawberry prunt.

10 *Façon de Venise glass*, Netherlandish. Mid-seventeenth century (Victoria and Albert Museum, London). Based on a Venetian model, it has in the convoluted stem threads of coloured glass, known as *'vitro di trina'*, and pincered wings.

11 *Façon de Venise glass*, possibly German. Mid-seventeenth century (Leslie Scott Antiques, London). Although less elaborate in design and decoration than 10, it was probably similarly intended for display rather than use.

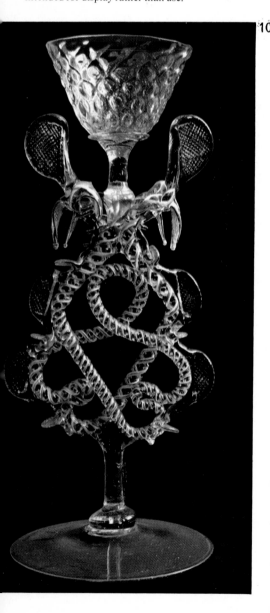

10

12 *Glass flask*, English. Late sixteenth or early seventeenth century (Victoria and Albert Museum, London). Roman glass has been discovered in England, but the origins of the English glass-making industry date from the thirteenth century.

13 *Four glass apothecaries' phials*, English. Seventeenth century (Victoria and Albert Museum, London). This green glass is comparable to the forest glass used for the *Stangenglas* in 8.

22

14

16

17

15

14–18 *Drinking-glasses*, English. *c.*1685–1715 (Private Collection). The earliest of these glasses (16, left) owes the inspiration for its design to Venice although, like the other examples, which are truly local in conception, it was made in England. This fact and the feature of a folded foot is all they have in common with one another, as each is completely different in appearance. While the bowls do not always vary greatly in shape, the stems exhibit their makers' artistry. The components, which are not many in number, were assembled in a multiplicity of different ways so that each wineglass has a personality of its own. Some types of stems are now much scarcer than others, the three in 18 being the rarest of those illustrated here.

18

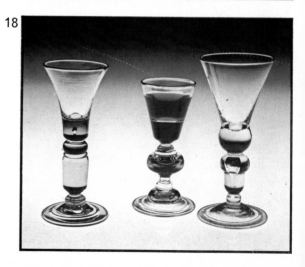

19–21 *Drinking-glasses*, English. *c.*1730–50 (Private Collection). All the glasses below have engraved bowls; also, they have the particularly graceful stems typical of Newcastle makers. Those in 19 and 20 have groups of air-bubbles in their stems. Dating from about 1750, it may be noticed that they lack the pre-1745 folded foot. This is to be seen in the two earlier plain-stemmed glasses of about 1730 in 21. The glass on the left of 21 is engraved with two men seated at a table drinking, and each holds his glass by the foot.

22–24 *Commemorative glasses*, English. Eighteenth century (Cecil Higgins Art Gallery, Bedford [23], and Private Collection). Glasses bearing on them commemorative designs or inscriptions have an especial interest, as they reveal something of the course of history. All those illustrated on this page are English, although the example on the left in 22 was engraved abroad. Next to it is a 'deceptive' glass with a very thick-walled bowl, used by toast-masters so that they could perform their duties drinking often but only in very small quantities. Like the example on the left in 23, it commemorates the Williamite cause. The opposing faction, the Jacobites are recognized by the glass engraved with a rose in 22 and the portrait of the Young Pretender on the right-hand glass in 23. The glasses in 24 are also Jacobite glasses, with the exception of the centre one. This bears the word 'LIBERTY' above the white horse from the arms of Hanover, Germany, which was ruled by the British sovereign.

23

22

24

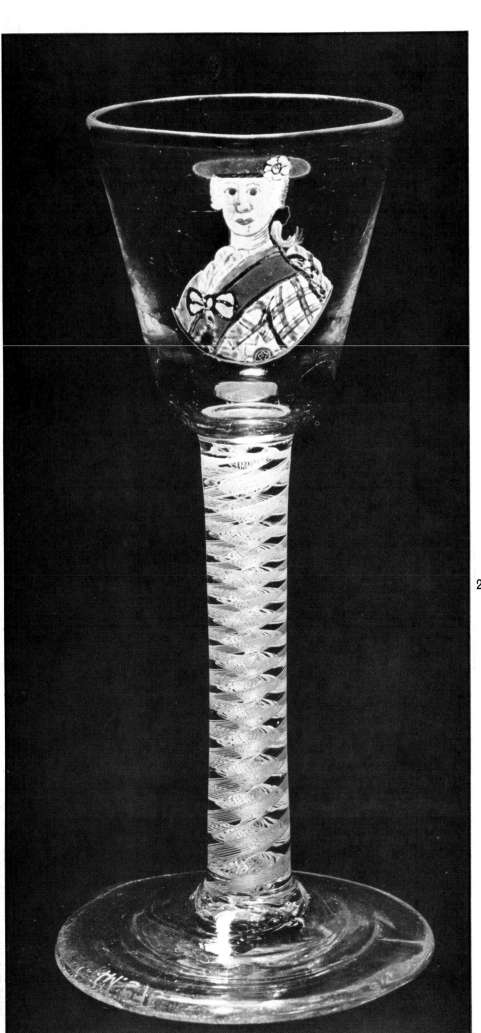

25 *Commemorative glass*, English. 1760s (Ashmolean Museum, Oxford). Enamelled with a portrait of the Young Pretender, the wineglass is smaller than shown. The rough execution of the painting contrasts with the neatness of the Beilbys' workmanship, as seen on the glass below and in 33.

26 *Wineglass*, decorated in enamel by a member of the Beilby family, Newcastle upon Tyne. 1760s (Victoria and Albert Museum, London). One of a pair, it is inscribed 'Eliz^th Smith; the other, which may have been executed for her husband or brother, bears the name Jn° Smith.

26

27 and 28 *Wine- and sweetmeat-glasses*, English. *c.*1714–50 (Private Collection). These all have flat-sided supports which swell as they rise, known as 'Silesian' stems. They are considered to have been introduced in about 1714, when George I came to England from Hanover to succeed Queen Anne on the throne. Very rare examples are moulded with the patriotic legend 'God Save King George', one word on the widest part of each facet, while others bear the initials G.R. and crowns. The first Silesian stems were four sided, but they became hexagonal in section from about 1720, octagonal some five years later and went out of production soon after the middle of the century.

29–31 *Air-twist glasses*, English. Mid-eighteenth century (Private Collection). The air-twist stem was introduced shortly before 1740. The ingenuity of the craftsmen did not rest at devizing the complex, thread-like, interior patterns, they extended their skills to inventing fresh combinations of knops and plain sections. The knop is not only a decoration, but it assisted those who gripped a glass by the stem in preference to holding it by the foot (see 21). The air-twist stem of the brilliant green glass in 30 is a refinement that is largely wasted in a coloured metal, where it scarcely shows up. The five wineglasses in 29 were all made in about 1750, but not all mid-eighteenth-century buyers shared the same taste. If they preferred a plain stem they could have selected some of the examples in 31, which were in the shops at about that time. The two glasses on the left are gilded and engraved, respectively, with vineleaves and bunches of grapes, while the next shows a gallant toasting a lady. The lettered example bears the words 'Success to Sir Francis Knollys' and is a relic of an election held at Reading in 1761. Sir Francis, incidentally, won the seat.

31

32

32 *Air-twist glasses with engraved bowls*, English. *c*.1750–60 (Private Collection). Some of them bear patterns of hops and barley (the first glass on the left and the three on the right), suggesting that they were used for ale. This was a much stronger drink in the past than it is today, and it would therefore have been taken in small quantities.

33 *Glasses with gilt and enamelled decoration*, English. *c*.1765–80 (Private Collection). The enamelled glasses are by William Beilby and his sister Mary. They include a squat tumbler painted with the arms of the Grand Lodge of England, which has a noticeably thick base and is known as a 'firing' glass. The name was acquired because they were banged on table-tops to applaud or call to order, and the noise resembled volleys of musket-fire.

33

34 *Incised-twist wineglasses*, English. *c.*1750–60 (Private Collection). Wineglass stems were not always decorated internally, as were the faceted Silesian stems in 27 and 28. The ones shown here are all incised on the outside, so that they look as if they have been wound round with transparent, thin string. Examples are not common, and they would seem to have been made only between about 1750 and 1765.

35 *Opaque-twist glasses*, English. 1760–75 (Private Collection). Their decoration was not formed by manipulating air-bubbles, as was the case with air twists, but by incorporating lengths of white glass in clear. Then they were pulled and twisted until the desired lace-like pattern was completed, and this was cut into stem-length sections for use. The bowls range from large-sized goblets to others holding very little. The third from the left is known as a 'ratafia flute' and was for drinking ratafia, a liqueur flavoured with almonds or with the kernels of peaches, apricots or cherries.

36

37

36 *Wineglasses*, English. *c.*1760–70 (Private Collection). By about 1760 air-twist stems had reached the height of their popularity and were being supplanted by the opaque twists, which in turn reached the height of fashion in about 1770. Occasionally the two types of ornamentation appear together, as here. The large example to the left of the group has a bowl patterned in a raised trellis-like design known a century earlier to George Ravenscroft. Then, he described it rather prettily as 'nipt diamond waies'.

37 *Engraved opaque-twist glasses*, English. *c.*1760–80 (Private Collection). Ale-glasses, of which six are shown here, have a capacity of three to four ounces and long and relatively narrow bowls. Cordial-glasses, of which two are illustrated, have small bowls on tall and extra-stout stems.

38 *Set of four salts and a tea-caddy with a silver lid*, Irish. The salts *c.*1780, the tea-caddy *c.*1800 (Cecil Davis Limited, London). There is in the National Museum of Ireland, Dublin, a document dated 1786 giving undoubted proof that coloured glass was made in Ireland. Written by the clerk at the Waterford concern, which had started three years earlier, it gives the recipes in use at the time for making 'Flint [Clear], Enamel [opaque white], blue and best Green Glass'.

39 *Cut-glass sugar-bowls*, Irish. *c.*1790 (Delomosne and Son Limited, London). A severe tax was imposed on English glass in 1781, causing non-dutiable Irish glass to gain popularity in Europe and encouraging an increase of activity in the Irish glass industry. It is often difficult to attribute a piece to a particular factory and it is sometimes difficult to distinguish Irish from English glass as English glass-workers and factory managers went to work in Ireland.

40 *Cut-glass bowl with 'turnover' rim*, Irish. *c.*1800 (Delomosne and Son Limited, London). Having a comparatively large surface area, bowls often received the most ambitious cut decoration. Because there was no tax on the weight of Irish glass, Irish vessels characteristically have thicker walls and deeper cut decoration than English ones.

41 *Goblet and cover*, Potsdam. Early eighteenth century (Victoria and Albert Museum, London). The art of glass-engraving reached a new brilliance in Bohemia at this time, emulating the skill of the lapidary. This goblet is embellished with gilding.

42 *Beaker and cover*, Bohemian. Early eighteenth century (Victoria and Albert Museum, London). The clear glass has ruby and 'aventurine' enclosures and it is wheel engraved. Ruby glass, here incorporated in a complex ribbon motif, was the invention of a Potsdam chemist named Johann Kunckel.

42

43 *Tea-bowl and saucer*, probably German. Mid-eighteenth century (British Museum, London). The opaque-white glass is decorated with enamelling to imitate contemporary Meissen or Vienna porcelain.

44 *Bottle or decanter*, German. Second half of the eighteenth century (Victoria and Albert Museum, London). Opaque-white glass, called 'milk-glass' was provided as a cheap alternative to European porcelain, first produced at Meissen in 1710.

43

45

44

46

47

45 *Zwischengold beaker*, German. Early eighteenth century (Victoria and Albert Museum, London). *Zwischengold* glasses are made up of two vessels which fit exactly one within the other, the etched gold-leaf decoration being enclosed between the two layers of glass.

46 *Zwischengold tumbler*, German. *c.*1720 (Victoria and Albert Museum, London). A rare, early version of *Zwischengoldglas*, the gold leaf covers the entire surface of the inner vessel while the inner surface of the outer vessel is enamelled to resemble marble.

47 *Tankard*, Ehrenfriedersdorf, Saxony. Early eighteenth century (Victoria and Albert Museum, London). The blue glass is wheel engraved and the lid is pewter.

48 *Wineglass*, decorated by Johann Friedrich Meyer, Dresden. Eighteenth century (Pilkington Glass Museum, St. Helens). The glass has a baluster stem and was decorated by one of the most illustrious of German glass-enamellers.

49 *Tumbler* by Johann Joseph Mildner (1763–1808), Guttenbrunn, Lower Austria. 1788 (British Museum, London). Mildner glasses have *Zwischengold* medallions inserted into their walls and bases, and in some cases they have narrow borders. The medallions depict allegorical and other subjects, including landscapes and still lifes, names and monograms, as well as inscriptions which are visible in the interiors of the pieces. The gold leaf, here on a red base, makes a fine contrast with the purity of the milk glass.

50 *Beaker or ice-pail*, probably Bohemian. *c*.1750–70 (British Museum, London). The opaque-white glass is enamelled with scenes depicting the Elements. The enamel and gilt decoration on milk-glass was usually executed by porcelain-decorators, who worked in a similar style on porcelain and glass.

49

50

51 *Wineglass-cooler* signed by Isaac Jacobs, Bristol. *c.*1800 (Victoria and Albert Museum, London). The Jacobs family ran a glass-house in Bristol between 1771 and 1806. These coolers were filled with cold water, into which were placed the bowls of wineglasses, the stems resting on the lips.

52 *Salt*, English. *c.*1800 (Victoria and Albert Museum, London). This could have been made at any of the glasshouses in England producing blue glassware; similar blue cut-glass salts were made in Ireland.

53 *Decanter for shrub*, English. Last quarter of the eighteenth century (Victoria and Albert Museum, London). Shrub is a cordial made from spirit, fruit juice and sugar. The decanter was probably manufactured in Bristol, where a number of similar blue-glass pieces were made. Zaffre, which produced the deep blue colour, arrived in England at Bristol and was distributed from there; hence the term 'Bristol Blue', applied indiscriminately to blue glass produced anywhere in the British Isles.

54 *Tea-canister*, probably south Staffordshire. *c.*1755–60 (Victoria and Albert Museum, London). Opaque-white glass was decorated in the same manner as ceramics of the period. In eighteenth-century England the description of 'enamel-painter' could mean a decorator on copper, pottery, porcelain or glass, and some artists worked with all these materials.

55 *Finger-bowl*, English. Late eighteenth century (Bristol City Art Gallery, Bristol). The green glass is decorated with a honeycomb decoration, each cell containing a gilt, heraldic ermine motif.

56 *Covered vase*, English. *c.*1760 (Victoria and Albert Museum, London). 10½ inches in height, this opaque-white vase in the form of a Chinese pot has enamelled decoration.

57 *Cruet-bottle with spire stopper*, probably decorated in the workshop of James Giles, Berwick Street, Soho. *c.*1765–70 (Victoria and Albert Museum, London). Giles, who had workshops in London and elsewhere, characteristically used lavish gilding in his decorations. Exotic birds standing on a pebble ground is a motif that he often used.

58 *Set of three decanters in a leather-covered stand*, the brandy and rum decanters signed 'I. Jacobs Bristol', the Holland decanter probably from a different set. Late eighteenth century (Bristol City Art Gallery, Bristol). Michael Edkins, a famous Bristol decorator, worked for the Jacobs factory between 1785 and 1787 and may have decorated these.

60

59

59 *Mug*, Egermann factory, Blottendorf, northern Bohemia. *c.*1830 (Richard Dennis, London). Dense black and sealing-wax red glasses were invented by Count George von Buquoy in 1822 and called 'Hyalith'. The following year Friedrich Egermann (1777–1864) started to produce wares in *Hyalith* at his glassworks. As milk-glass was developed in Bohemia in imitation of Meissen and Vienna porcelain, so the black *Hyalith* was used in the manner of Wedgwood's black basaltes.

60 *Jug*, Egermann factory, Blottendorf, northern Bohemia. *c.*1820 (Victoria and Albert Museum, London). *Lithyalin*, a marbled glass produced in a remarkable range of glowing colours, was invented by Egermann after *Hyalith*.

61 *Covered goblet and beaker*, Bohemian. The goblet *c.*1850, the beaker *c.*1825 (Richard Dennis, London). The engraving of the goblet is in the manner of Karl Pfohl. Seven panels on the opposite surface reflect the startled horse in miniature. These reflecting panels are found only on the highest quality engraved glass. The beaker has five panels, four with views of Baden and the fifth bearing the name of its original owner. In the first half of the nineteenth century souvenir glass engraved with portraits and landscapes was very popular with visitors to European spas.

62 *Scent-bottle and stopper*, Bohemian. *c.*1830–40 (Bethnal Green Museum, London). Egermann's *Lithyalin* is here used to great effect. Like *Hyalith*, it was sometimes gilded and painted, and it was much used for all types of useful wares.

61

65

63 *Beaker*, Bohemian. *c.*1830–40 (Victoria and Albert Museum, London). The wide range of colours that was produced in *Lithyalin* is shown here. Glass had imitated precious and semi-precious stones since antiquity, but never before with such boldness.

64 *Goblet*, Bohemian. *c.*1840 (Victoria and Albert Museum, London). The glass is cut and engraved through a layer of yellow stain. Glass stained purple was popular in the eighteenth century; in the nineteenth century vivid red, green, and yellow stains became popular. The chunky form of the goblet is characteristic of glass produced in the Biedermeier period, between about 1815 and 1848.

65 *Vase*, Bohemian. *c.*1830–40 (Victoria and Albert Museum, London). The glass is cut and engraved on the wheel and has yellow and pink stains and silvering. This is a fine example of Biedermeier glass and it indicates the type of solid, gaudy ware that appealed to the middle classes.

66 *Mug*, Imperial or Bakhmet'yev Glass Factory, Russia. *c.*1814. From the late seventeenth century Russia followed western styles and fashions in the manufacture of glass; the opaque-white glass of the mug is akin to a European glass made in imitation of porcelain. It is painted with a caricature of Napoleon and the meaning of the inscription is that Napoleon failed to make the Russians dance to his tune and was forced to dance to theirs.

63

64

66

42

67 *Covered vase*, possibly by Thomas Hawkes. Late 1830s (Victoria and Albert Museum, London). The glass is double walled, the outer layer cut, the inner layer painted and gilt. An elaborate William IV or early Victorian confection, it combines a number of different techniques.

68 *Claret-jug*, a cut-glass decanter with silver mounts by Benjamin Smith, Jun., of Duke Street, Lincoln's Inn Fields. Hallmarked London 1841–42 (Victoria and Albert Museum, London). The adaptation of the decanter to a claret-jug is achieved with a vine motif; the handle is the vine stem.

69 *Standing bowl*, probably by James Powell and Sons, London. *c.*1851 (Victoria and Albert Museum, London). In 1845 the duty on glass was abolished and the English glass-makers were at last in a position to compete with foreign makers.

70 *Wine-cooler*, English or Irish. *c.*1815–25 (Victoria and Albert Museum, London). The deep mitre-cutting, so different from the delicate cutting of the previous century, makes the piece comparable to the weighty Biedermeier glass produced contemporaneously in central Europe.

71 *Goblet*, probably Stourbridge. *c.*1845–50 (Victoria and Albert Museum, London). The opaque-white glass has a painted decoration. By this time Stourbridge, in Worcestershire, had become the centre of the English glass trade.

72 *Water-jug* by W. H., B. and J. Richardson, Stourbridge. 1848 (Victoria and Albert Museum, London). Many Victorian glasses can be attributed and dated by reference to pattern-books and public and company records; the design of this jug was registered in 1848.

73 *Carafe*, designed by Richard Redgrave R.A., for Henry Cole's Summerly's Art Manufactures and made by J. F. Christy, Lambeth. 1847 (Victoria and Albert Museum, London). Summerly's Art Manufactures commissioned designs and sold them to manufacturers of silver, china and glass; they were paid a royalty on sales. Redgrave designed for them a series of carafes and glasses with a painted decoration of tall leaves, apparently growing from the gilt base in this example. The designs were on the whole quite unlike any others produced at the time, but they were not particularly popular.

74 *Wineglasses*, English. *c.*1840 (Delomosne and Son Limited, London). The green glass bears an engraved decoration.

71

72

73

74

75 *Two champagne-glasses* by George Bacchus and Sons, Birmingham. *c.*1830 (Victoria and Albert Museum, London). Their looped stems are obviously imitative of Venetian and *façon de Venise* glass, though attached to an entirely different shape of bowl.

76 *Two goblets*, English. Nineteenth century (Victoria and Albert Museum, London). The one on the left was made at the Davenport factory, Longport, in about 1815; the one on the right was, according to the date engraved beneath the initials 'CA', made in 1840. Both are wheel engraved. Sturdy drinking-glasses in the early nineteenth-century tradition were made throughout the Victorian period.

46

77

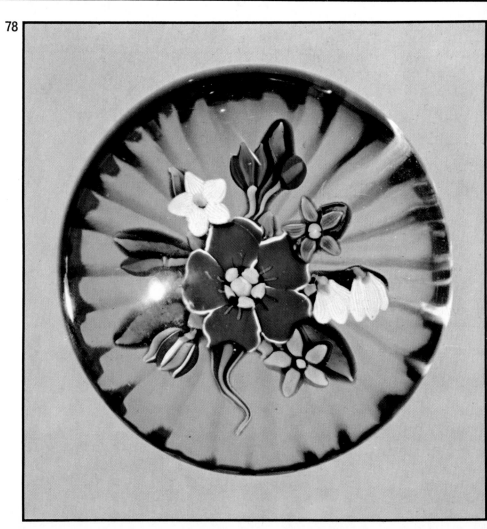

78

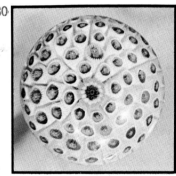

77 *Crown Imperial paperweight*, Baccarat. Nineteenth century (Spink and Son Limited, London). Baccarat – La Compagnie des Cristalleries Baccarat – was the largest of the French glassworks at this time. Manufacturers of fine crystal glassware, they turned to the production of glass paperweights in 1846, when trade was poor. This excessively rare example is three inches in diameter.

78 *Bouquet paperweight*, St. Louis. Nineteenth century (Spink and Son Limited, London). St. Louis devoted a considerable proportion of its production of paperweights to flowers, fruit, vegetables and reptiles. Compared with those from Baccarat and Clichy, St. Louis weights are generally more delicately coloured.

79 *Camomile paperweight*, St. Louis. Nineteenth century (Spink and Son Limited, London). Most single flowers are set in clear glass. French paperweights were little valued at the beginning of this century, but their popularity has increased considerably in recent years.

80 *Millefiori paperweight*, St. Louis. Nineteenth century (Spink and Son Limited, London). In May 1845 Pietro Bigaglia, a Venetian glass-maker, displayed his *millefiori* paperweights at the Exhibition of Austrian Industry in Vienna. They were noticed by Eugène Peligot, a professor at the French Conservatoire National des Arts et Métiers, who recommended that they should be manufactured in France. Though the idea originated in Italy, Italian paperweights were inferior in quality to the French ones.

82

81

83

81 *Bouquet paperweight*, Clichy. Nineteenth century (Spink and Son Limited, London). The Cristalleries de Clichy was situated in a village outside Paris. Their hallmark is the so-called 'Clichy rose', of which two appear in this bouquet. Occasionally the weights are marked with a 'C' and still more rarely the whole word 'Clichy'.

82 *Millefiori garland paperweight*, Clichy. Nineteenth century (Spink and Son Limited, London). The canes which form *millefiori* glass are welded together, arranged in a pattern and picked up by a ball of molten glass from the furnace on a pontil rod; the pontil mark is later smoothed flat.

83 *Beaker*, French. *c*.1810 (Richard Dennis, London). The semi-transparent glass known as 'opaline' was first made in France. A type of luxury glass, in the Empire period it was made into simple forms, usually of classical derivation. It was originally produced in a pure milky white, but rose pink, apple green and turquoise opaline soon became fairly common.

84 *Butterfly paperweight*, Baccarat. Nineteenth century (Spink and Son Limited, London). A butterfly was the subject of four per cent of all Baccarat weights; the body of the creature is always blue or purple and the wings multi-coloured.

85 *Ewer and bowl*, French. *c*.1830 (Kunstindustrimuseet, Oslo). The opaline vessels are mounted with gilt-bronze; much of the finest opaline is similarly mounted, giving it a graceful appearance.

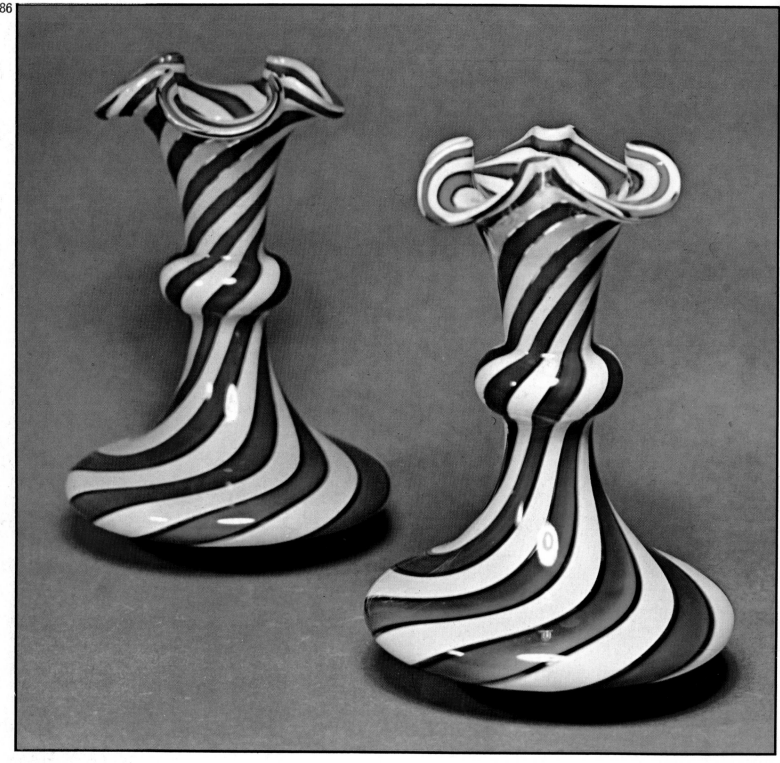

86 *Pair of vases*, probably St. Louis. *c.*1850 (Kunstindustrimuseet, Oslo). From the Venetians the French learnt to use brilliantly coloured glass in stripes and spirals, as well as the technique of making *millefiori* glass, but the quality and weight of their glass was entirely different: the French never adopted the brittle, lightweight metal which enabled the Venetians to produce their intricately decorated glass.

87 *Glass fountain with birds and deer*, probably Nailsea. Early nineteenth century (Clevedon Court, Somerset. National Trust). In 1788 a glassworks was established in the village of Nailsea, near Bristol, which, by the beginning of the nineteenth century, had begun to specialize in the production of ornamental coloured glass. The factory closed in 1873. Today, 'Nailsea glass' tends to refer to a style rather than a place of origin.

88 *Striped carafe and tumbler and green glass hat and cider-jug*, Nailsea. Nineteenth century (Clevedon Court, Somerset. National Trust). The striped glass may have been made by French glassworkers, reputed to have lived in a row of cottages in Nailsea called 'French rank'. The hat is probably an apprentice's piece.

89 *Three bottles*, probably Nailsea. Early nineteenth century (Clevedon Court, Somerset. National Trust). Flecked glass was a speciality at Nailsea. Until 1845 flint glass was heavily taxed and, as green bottle-glass bore less duty, it is probable that Nailsea worked with bottle-glass as an economy, using flecks of enamel colour to alleviate the drabness.

90 *Two rolling-pins*, English. Mid-nineteenth century (Sotheby and Co., London). Between 1830 and 1860, glass rolling-pins were at their most popular and Nailsea was one of the principal places of manufacture. These two were probably made at Nailsea.

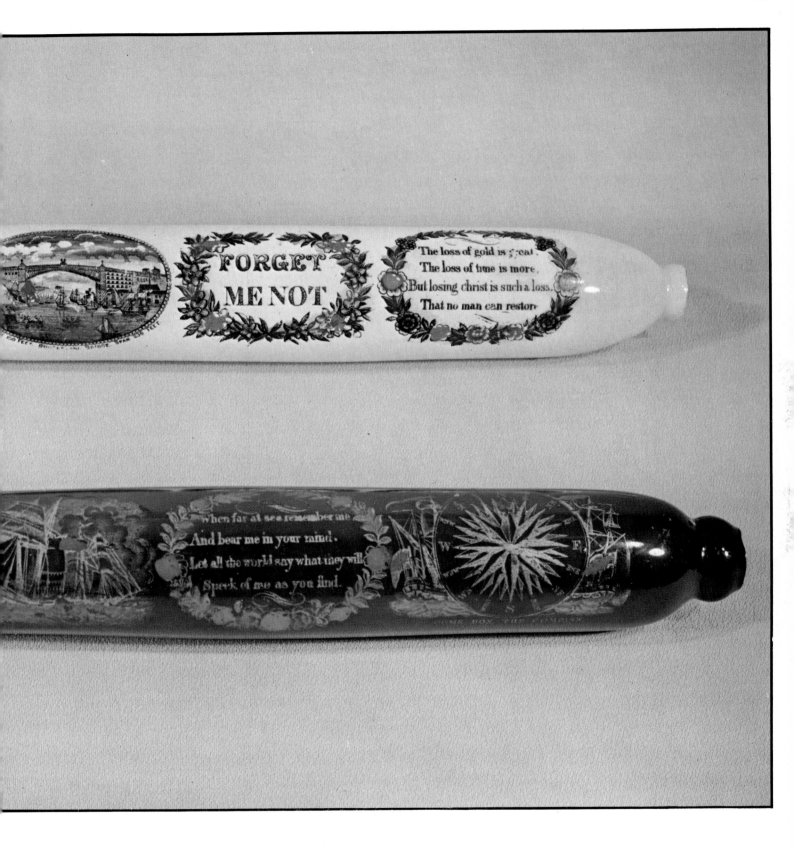

91

92

91 *Rolling-pin*, English. Mid-nineteenth century (Sotheby and Co., London). Commemorative rolling-pins were sometimes given as wedding and christening presents.

92 *Rolling-pin*, English. Mid-nineteenth century (Sotheby and Co., London). Glass curiosities such as rolling-pins, walking-sticks, dumps (door stops), bells, pipes and rolling-pins were known at Nailsea as 'friggers'.

93 *Vase*, Thomas Webb and Sons. *c.*1880 (Alan Tillman Antiques, London). Cameo glass, such as this, was the revival of a technique known to the Romans. It was inspired by the Portland Vase, a glass vase of the first century AD copied by Wedgwood in pottery. Today, cameo glass is much sought after by collectors.

94 *Vase*, by Joshua Hodgetts (1857–1933) for Stevens and Williams. *c.*1890 (Stourbridge Town Council Collection, Worcestershire). Hodgetts was a knowledgeable amateur botanist and on this commercial piece in the shape of an Indian vessel he allowed his enthusiasm to emerge. Cameo glass is a form of cased, or flashed, glass. Two layers of glass are usually used, the overlay generally being white. When produced commercially, the decoration was achieved first by treating the appropriate areas with acid and then finishing it with an engraving-wheel. Early, non-commercial pieces were carved entirely by hand.

93

95 *Vase*, designed by Thomas Woodall (1849–1926) and cut by J. T. Fereday for Thomas Webb and Sons. 1884 (Victoria and Albert Museum, London). This was made for the 1884 International Health Exhibition, at which Thomas Woodall won a bronze medal for his vases and bowls.

96 *Vase and scent-bottle*, probably by Thomas Webb and Sons. *c.*1890 (Richard Dennis, London). The firm of Webb, apart from producing cameo glass such as this, also manufactured glass in imitation of carved ivory, the first twenty pieces of which were acquired by Queen Victoria.

97 *Four scent-bottles*, Thomas Webb and Sons. *c.*1880 (Alan Tillman Antiques, London). Much cameo glass has a matt surface.

96

95

97

98   *Vase*, by George Woodall. 1910 (Stourbridge Town Council Collection, Worcestershire). The scene depicted is The Origin of Painting. Much of the most remarkable cameo glass was made for the numerous international exhibitions of the nineteenth century; this one was made for the Brussels Exhibition of 1911.

99   *Vase*, by John Northwood (1836–1902). Late nineteenth century (Science Museum, London). Also shown is an assortment of tools used by Northwood for the cutting and engraving of cameo glass. He was the first glass-maker in England to produce cameo glass on a classical pattern. One of his greatest achievements was a replica of the Portland Vase.

100   *Bowl*, designed and cut by Jacob Face for Thomas Webb and Sons. 1884 (Victoria and Albert Museum, London). Like the vase designed by Thomas Woodall for Thomas Webb and Sons (95), this was made specifically for display at the International Health Exhibition.

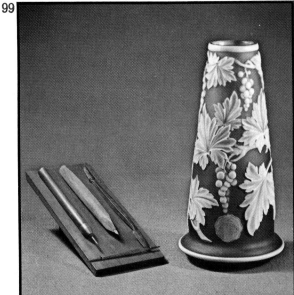

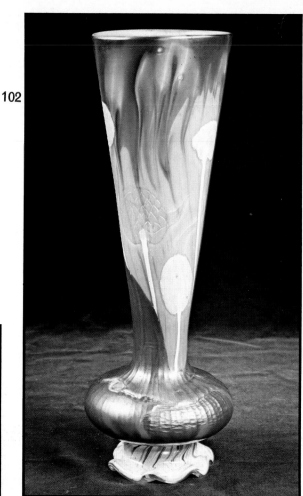

101 *Figure of Loïe Fuller*, by Amalric Walter. After 1906 (Alain Lesieutre Collection). Loïe Fuller was an American dancer who originated the serpentine dance in Paris; in 1906 Amalric Walter signed a contract with the Daum company to use their kilns for firing pieces associated with Loïe Fuller. This is executed in *pâté-de-verre*, a process revived by Henri Gros. Crushed glass fragments are mixed with coloured oxides, placed in a mould and fired. The cooled paste can then be modelled with a spatula.

102 *Vase*, by Emile Gallé (1846–1904). *c.*1900 (Alain Lesieutre Collection). Gallé was one of the principal Art Nouveau designers in France and the guiding light of the Nancy School of craftsmen. Originally he was interested only in hand-made non-commercial processes such as the *marquetrie de verre* of this vase. The process involved pressing pieces of semi-molten glass into the surface of the vessel before it was cooled. It was so difficult to achieve that many pieces were cracked in the making.

103 *Bowl*, by Joseph Brocard. *c.*1900 (N. Manoukian Collection). Brocard was one of the many artists of the period living in Paris and London who was fascinated by Middle and Far Eastern art. An example of his later and rarely seen work, the bowl has a delicacy in the decoration that is obviously Eastern in spirit.

104 *Vase*, Daum Frères, Nancy. *c.*1900 (Sotheby and Co., London). The milky-blue glass is overlaid with blue-grey and carved with a thorn pattern; the mount is of gilt bronze set with glass drops.

105 *Dragonfly vase*, by Emile Gallé (1846–1904). *c.*1900 (Musée des Arts Décoratifs, Paris). The French Art Nouveau glass-makers were in the practice of signing their work, thereby implying that each piece was unique and worthy of individual attention. Even with his commercial pieces, Gallé was determined to show that it was possible to reconcile cheap production with art.

106 *Bowl*, Daum Frères, Nancy. 1900–6 (John Jesse Collection). The firm of Daum Frères made a speciality after 1893 of acid-cut glass. This bowl has also enamel-painted decoration. Their decorative motifs were usually sprays of flowers, fruit, wild grasses or landscapes.

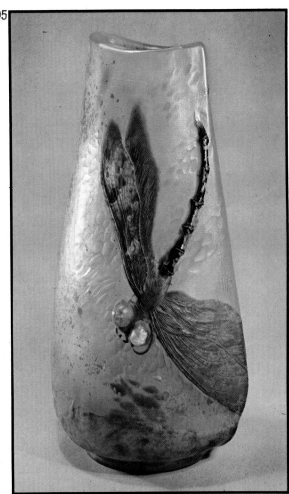

105

106

107 *Vase*, James Couper and Sons, Glasgow. *c.*1885–1905 (Private Collection). The firm of Couper and Sons were the original producers of Clutha glass. 'Clutha' is an old Scottish word meaning 'cloudy'.

108 *Vase*, Couper and Sons, Glasgow. *c.*1885–1905 (Private Collection). Clutha glass is recognizable by the bubbled and streaked effect of its surface.

109 *Four-handled bottle*, designed by Christopher Dresser (1834–1904) for Couper and Sons, Glasgow. Late nineteenth century (Victoria and Albert Museum, London). This has Couper's flower mark on the base and the words 'Clutha designed by C.D.' Dresser was a prominent Victorian designer, whose taste for simplicity and uncluttered, unornamented forms was quite at variance with his contemporaries. He was strongly influenced by Japanese design.

110 *Vase*, designed by George Walton (1867–1933). 1896–98 (Victoria and Albert Museum, London). George Walton was a Glasgow architect and interior decorator who, for about two years, designed Clutha glass for James Couper and Sons.

111 *Three vases*, designed by Max von Spaun, Lötz, Klostermühle. *c.*1900 (Private Collection). Iridescent glass was first displayed at the International Exhibition in Vienna in 1873. It was exhibited by the Austrian glassmaker Lobmeyr and copied immediately by Thomas Webb and Sons of Stourbridge. Tiffany, in New York, drew on Webb's experience and in turn one of his glassworkers took the secret to the firm of Lötz in Bohemia. Von Spaun, a brilliant businessman as well as designer, took over the Lötz factory in 1879 and, producing wares that were often indubitable copies of Tiffany designs, created a flourishing trade in iridescent glass.

112 *Four vases*, Lötz, Klostermühle. *c.*1900 (Victoria and Albert Museum, London, and Private Collection). The origin of iridescent glass is sometimes ascribed to the year 1850 when, in the Hungarian town of Zlatno, fireworks were exploded in a furnace during a festival. Iridescent wares were made at several other European factories and, since few Lötz pieces are signed, attributions are often difficult.

114

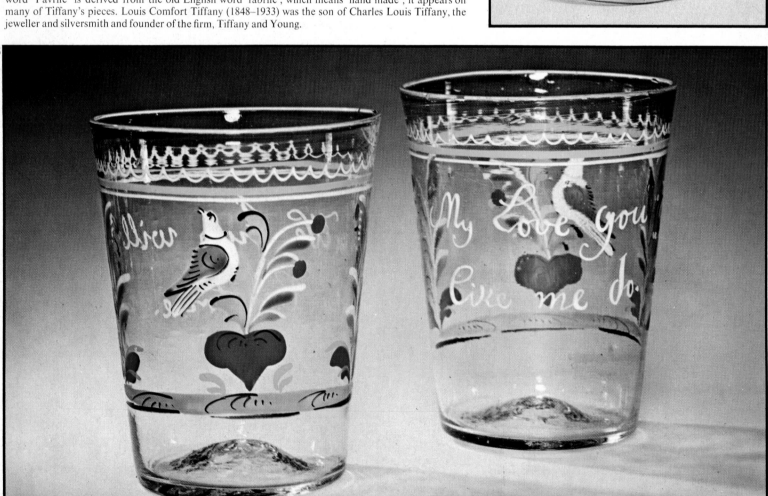

113 *Two tumblers*, probably made in Europe and enamelled at Stiegel's glassworks, Mannheim. 1772–74 (Corning Museum of Glass, New York). The American colonies began to develop an independent glass industry in the mid-eighteenth century. Henry William Stiegel (1729–1785), born in Cologne, arrived in America in 1750 and practised first as an iron-worker. His was the first glasshouse in America to make fine tableware in emulation of European glass, to which it bears a great similarity. He also imported European glass and decorated it with the local market in mind. He died bankrupt.

114 *Candle-holder*, Mount Washington Glass Company, 1885–95 (Corning Museum of Glass, New York). Burmese glass, of which this is an example, is an opaque glass containing gold and uranium oxides which cause the change in hue from pale yellow to pink. It is one of the many different types of American glass known as 'art' glass, patented in the latter part of the nineteenth century. Queen Victoria was sent a tea-set in 'Queen's Burmese' pattern as a gift and Thomas Webb and Sons was licensed to produce it in England; this gives some indication of its original popularity.

115 *Paperweight vase*, Tiffany, New York. *c*.1900 (Sotheby's Belgravia, London). The decoration is trapped between two layers of tinted glass, giving the illusion of great depth. The finest paperweight vases were of this type, with sliced and embedded *millefiori* canes of a kind used in the traditional French paperweights. It is six inches in height and engraved on the base is '8520 N.L.C. Tiffany Inc. Favrile'. The word 'Favrile' is derived from the old English word 'fabrile', which means 'hand made'; it appears on many of Tiffany's pieces. Louis Comfort Tiffany (1848–1933) was the son of Charles Louis Tiffany, the jeweller and silversmith and founder of the firm, Tiffany and Young.

113

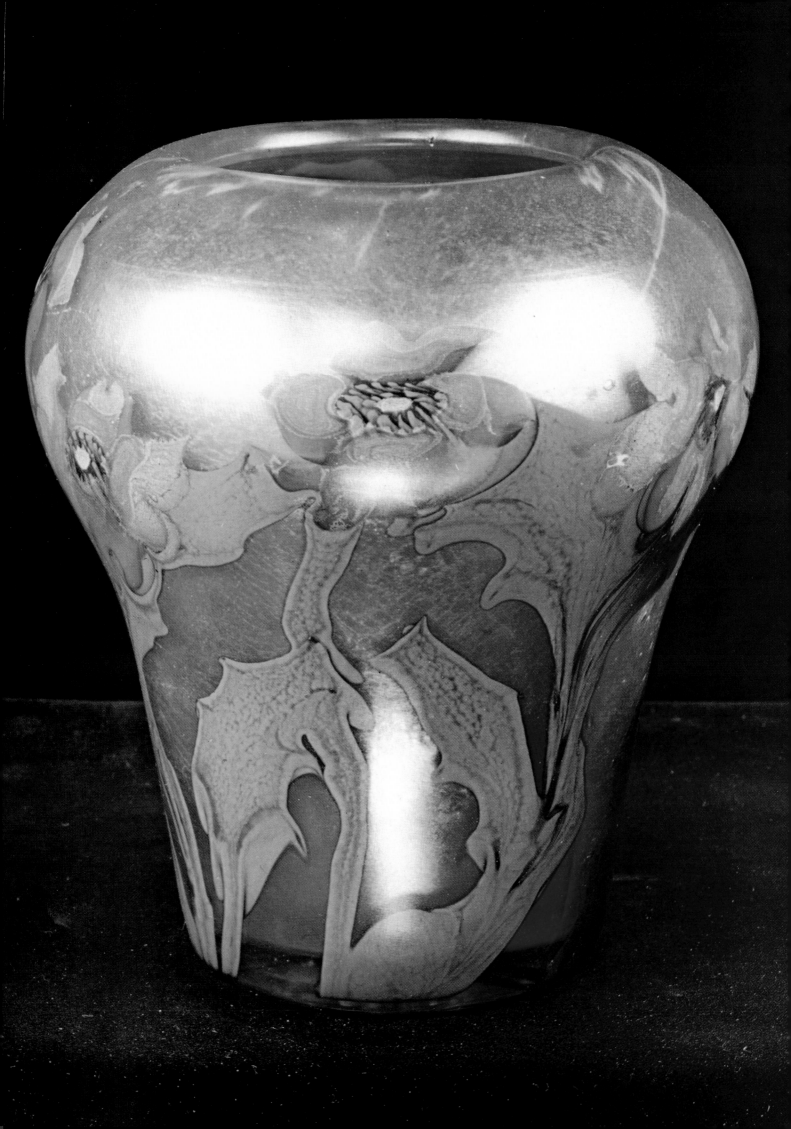

116

118

116 *Vase*, Tiffany. *c.*1900 (Sotheby's Belgravia, London). A speciality of Tiffany's was decorate iridescent ware. This pale green lustre vase is decorated with a trailing band of 'lily-pads' in high blue gold iridescence over black inlaid glass. Ancient glass held a particular fascination for Tiffany. He love the pitted, corroded effects caused by decomposition while it lay buried, and his ambition was t simulate these accidental imperfections. He also felt strongly that decoration should be integral to.th glass body; not applied to it at a later stage in its production. When the glass had cooled, the piece w finished.

117 *Wisteria lamp*, Tiffany Studios. *c.*1900 (Sotheby's Belgravia, London). Tiffany, before devotir himself entirely to the design and production of glass, worked as an interior decorator. He w therefore well aware of the strength of impression an object could make on its surroundings. His series lamps are an adaptation of the principles of stained glass.

118 *Flower vase*, Tiffany. *c.*1900 (Sotheby's Belgravia, London). The vase *is* a flower, as the lamp on t left *is* a wistaria. The combination of a naturalistic form with a function is one of Tiffany's principal ar most original theories. He also admired asymmetry, detesting the regular shapes and decoration nineteenth-century moulded and cut glass. His taste was for the exotic and luxurious, reflecting Ne York taste of his day. Though spurning simplicity, he advocated a return to natural forms, and in th sense he conforms to the many-sided ideal of an Art Nouveau designer.